ISSUE
PARADOX
ONE

Copyright © Rad Press Publishing

All artists maintain rights to their work.
All rights reserved. No part of this publication may be reproduced, distributed or conveyed, without the permission of the publisher.

First printing: 2016

ISBN 9780692752326

Cover design/Interior design by Mitch Green

BOARD OF ARTISTS

Ashley O'Melia
Jeremy Tolbert
Brandon Tomlinson
LR Poetess
Allison Profeta
Tania Brown
Josh Dale
April Green
Thom Young
RD Johnson
Emma Charlton
Ryan Vallee
Cassie Ferraro
Randy Mascorro
Allison Greenlee
Joe Adomavicia
Brande Mcclees
Wimana Chadband
Luna Magazine
Valorie Ruiz
Almaz Azmi
Arnab Bose
The Typist
Charmaine Landwehr
Gloria Linares
Huma Adnan
The girl with Kaleidoscope Heart
S.W. Collins
Kolleen Rianne
Rhett Pritchard
Samantha Lasky
Shannon Wiltshire
Victor Forna
Sarah Murdock
Harry Howard
Mackenzie Mullen
Neithan Levi
Ramsha Zubairi

You were more than just the oxygen I breathed, you were the beauty I saw in every dark haunting thought.

The Luna Zine
Gia - Sia Jane

Sweater Party
Brandon Tomlinson

A denim dress, stitched with holly branches
is what she showed up in.
Layered over the red turtle neck.

Sharing a whiskey and coke,
I stepped outside to get high.
Trying to catch my nerves.
Trying to calm my breath.

As guests began to lessen
we entered the room with the grey walls
and a book shelf storing Kierkegaard and Wilde.

Inching ever closer
in my bedroom
at my parents house,
no longer was she just a girl at
the sweater party.

Washed Away With a Whisper
Allison Profeta

My skin crawls sometimes. A burning unease. Buzzing like tattoo needles. Etching in my sins just below the surface. Just out of sight from everyone else. Taunting. Unsettled pacing. My hands pulling through my hair. My fingers pounding at the keys. Tears tightrope across my lashes. My soul aflame. My heart a kick drum rhythm. Aching. Play with me.

I beg.
Weak.
And needy.

Desperate for quiet. A quiet that hovers just out of reach. Always. Just below the surface. Just out of sight from everyone else A screaming specter only I can see. Threatening me I can't get free. Play with me. And when he does I beg. Weak And needy. Push me further. Make it hurt More. Quiet the burning and buzzing. That you can't hear. That you don't see Break me please Make me free And then Sometimes. The quiet comes unexpectedly Minus the pain Before I ever beg. Sometimes it's all washed away with a whisper. Make them sick with wanting to know what that feels like For just a moment. Without a struggle.

I'm set free

Love, Love, Love
Victor Forna

What haven't I seen son?
Sinned beneath this sun, sun, sun.
My skin has been burned, but my heart still loves.
My heart still loves. My heart still loves, loves, loves.
Sing her a song. Name a star after her.
Forever kiss, write a poem, break a heart.
Play with her tits. Jerk off your dick.
Watch porn, smoke weed forever. Kiss forever.
Love forever, fuck forever bliss.
The sun only burns now.
Only burns now.
Only burns now, now, now.
Tomorrow may die, read your damn notes.
Make jokes about your teacher's ass.
Take your girl far, far, and lie, lie,
lie to her about god, the universe,
souls, dreams, bones, sins,
insecurities.

Her insecurities made her mine.
Made her mine.
Made her mine, mine, mine.
Made her mine.
Be free like a madman at congo cross,
playing with his balls.
Unafraid of the sierra leonean sun,
or the screams of the sane.
Freedom is a sin.
Only you can forgive yourself.
Religion is not god.
There is a god.
Pray where you feel holy.
A room, a bottle, a woman, a poem.
Pray where you feel holy.
Death is not free.
Love what you love.
Hate who you hate, and do all of this with passion.
Passion will keep you going.
Will keep you going.
Will keep you going, going, going.
Don't let society kill it for one shit.
Don't let society chain you.
Be motherfucking free, till the birds and the stars,
and the waves, and the birds, and the winds
grow jealous of your freeness, of your wings.

Be free.

Forget Her
Jeremy Tolbert

At night
I see pearls in your smile
once the sky up above is
thrown away by the undressed
burgundy rain.
when that happens, the tears I
tried on yesterday
melt away
from the flames that
taste like ash.

enough for the clouds to fly away,
toying with my insides-
I collapse against the mirror
when I see it has all been just a dream.
so, I look upwards.
wading in the dirt of
a disgraced illusion
that has cast aside anything
resembling my eyes.
that is why I've mutilated my skin
for the milk of the women
who I've turned a slave to.

praising suicide,
I see you've moved with grace,
without me pulling at the purity
of your beauty.
I've tried to forget you somehow,
taking another drag from my killing machine.
yet, all along, I've been lost
without the addicted tar
that keeps me weak in the knees
taking me back to the moment we met--
up against the glistened, rain dropped wall
attached to the decaying street corner.
with my tears blanketing the city,
I am saddened that i've become
too sober to remember
the heartbeat that once was,
before it became a shadowed memory,
hovered over my now
broken and blackened heart.
I'd need a surgeon's blade
to lift up and expose the nothing
I have left inside.

Heat

Ashley O'Melia

I stare at the mud flaps of the semi in front of me, which immediately gives me the sensation of licking chocolate cake batter off my mom's rubber spatula when I was a kid. It is my only pleasant thought on a hot day like this, when a ten minute trip to the post office is like a journey into Death Valley. The only thing I can taste is not chocolate cake batter, but the dust and exhaust that chokes the air. The traffic moves with stilted sluggishness through this mix of residential and commercial areas, tall weeds spraying out around rusted porch railings next to the freshly asphalted parking lots of doctors and insurance agents. The sun slowly bakes the city, chasing its residents indoors and burnishing the skin of those who don't obey. It bounces off the concrete, granite, glass, and metal, and bores its lasers into my eyes despite my sunglasses. This drive is too short for the air conditioner to kick in on my old Subaru, so I drive with the windows down, hopeful for any breeze. I catch clips of songs and snatches of conversations as other folks drive by. "Why do you always..." "...breaking my heart..." "Can we get popsicles today, Mommy?" my daughter asks from the backseat. "Maybe." I glance at her in the rearview. Her porcelain skin has already flushed a bright pink and minute beads of sweat stand out along her hairline despite her tank top and shorts. She's playing with the map of Illinois she found in the pocket on the back of the seat. Locating our town and those of relatives has quickly become her favorite travel game. At six years old, she can read just about everything on it, but she can't quite fold it back up the right way. I don't mind. The true answer to the popsicle question is yes. I can't help but think about how the heat of the country is so different. The humidity is certainly worse, like a blanket from the dryer when it hasn't finished running its cycle yet. The cicadas protest angrily with their collective scream against the rising heat and their inevitable deaths, but their sound means life to me. The heat slowly warms the freshly-tilled earth and coaxes the seedlings out of their hard little cases. It stirs the catfish and bluegill from the bottom of the lake and beckons them to rise up to eat, beginning the fishing season. They gulp at the insects that skim across the silvery surface of the water and leave only concentric ripples in their wake. The oak trees unfurl their hand-like leaves eagerly to catch the rays of the sun, waving their pointy fingertips. The country absorbs the heat into its thick greenery. The breeze flows through the shady spots and feels like my grandmother's cool hand on my forehead. The heat is something completely different outside the city. With a sigh, I step out of my hot car and into the hotter parking lot of the post office. I'm sure my feet will melt right out of my flip flops and into the asphalt if we take too long. The lonely, hollow whine of police sirens ricochets off the brick building and funnels into my ears. I help my daughter from the backseat, and we rush toward the frigid air conditioning that we know is waiting inside.

Sing

Jeremy Tolbert

Sing, sing.
sing for me
before I bring
up the bones
soaked deep
in your belly.

I'm strung out
on the powder
of blood, This poisonous
light blinds us for life,
dancing around inside
our maze of veins.
Laying on broken
floorboards, inside,
underneath a parasol
because my eyelids
sizzle and crack.
Burnt nearly to the
ground, the view
I have ahead
of me are of a slough
of the young; bastards
lined up to get their fix.
Oh, where have all their
conscious crickets gone?
Because this aroma of
dying flesh have dissolved
into the walls. After watching
you kiss the chest of
someone up on church steps,
I tie up my strength with
radio wire, where the
memories of my past vanish
in what is left of the inside

of my nostrils.

Day Planner Elegies
Tania Brown

We braid the strands
of our stories into
emotional nooses
and hang our redemption.
Blood of sentiment
trickles from the
lacerations of constant
verbal flogging, the cane
of words soaked in
salty water adding
weight to the sting,
splitting flesh to render
judgement. Will we
ever be enough
for ourselves?
We lay blame at
our feet like tinder,
and light the match
with our anger.
Flames of our exaggerated
expectations make
our days a funeral pyre,
extended elegies written
in day planners recount
the hours spent reaching
for the perfection
we laid beyond grasp.

Home

April Green

I remember I used to climb inside him and lie amongst the clouds. Inhaling the scent of belonging. The taste of another world. And I would watch the silver lining beneath his skin moving with his breath. Rising like a silk parachute. Falling like a sprinkling of stardust. And I never found another place like him again. I never found another world like him again.

New Year's Eve

Brandon Tomlinson

Wearing the black
dress I loved.
Midnight was near.
Fading away further
than you can handle.

Hearing the voices
in their conversations.
Lost and you were
not coming back.
So, we left
without a toast.

In my car,
you felt as if
you were dying
and as the sky was
torched with color,
you came back to

start the year reborn.

Metamorphosis
Brande Mcclees

You wreak havoc
on all of my senses.
I cannot get past
the past
and the taste
of wasted time
on my tongue.
It's similar to
the bitterness
of burned garlic
and I often wonder
if I'll ever get
over it.

Your absence makes me question
what I want to do,
who I want to be,
and wonder why I'm wasting
my time by not working
toward my goals.
I want to sweep all
of my sorrows
and regrets into
the corner and cover
them with my doubts.
But most days
I lack the
courage to take
such a bold step.

You make me want to
eat all of my fears.
To simply swallow them whole
without a sip of libation.
Maybe then I could
Summon the nerve to
gather a strong gale beneath
My wings, disregard my trepidation,
and take
that leap.
In the hopes that
I'll be able to

Fly.

Second-hand Smoke
Ryan Valle

I have ashtrays
that fill like firepits
building smoke
and pushing fumes
and I've had no luck
burning you
clean

from my skin

His-ness
Tania Brown

Oceans erode my resistance, drop by drop. I tell them that missing him is really only me missing myself, that he is nothing—was nothing— that I am stronger than my memories. I will overcome old dreams bathed in the hazy light of recollection, a silk scarf tossed over a lamp to obscure the fine lines of pain and age. I can love those ideas of him uprooted from him— he doesn't need to feature— the tendrils covered in thoughts of soil, separate from the ground, distinct from the trunk.

Somewhere his his-ness resides and it alights my me-ness. I can forgive him everything for that; I can abide his absence,

he gave me myself.

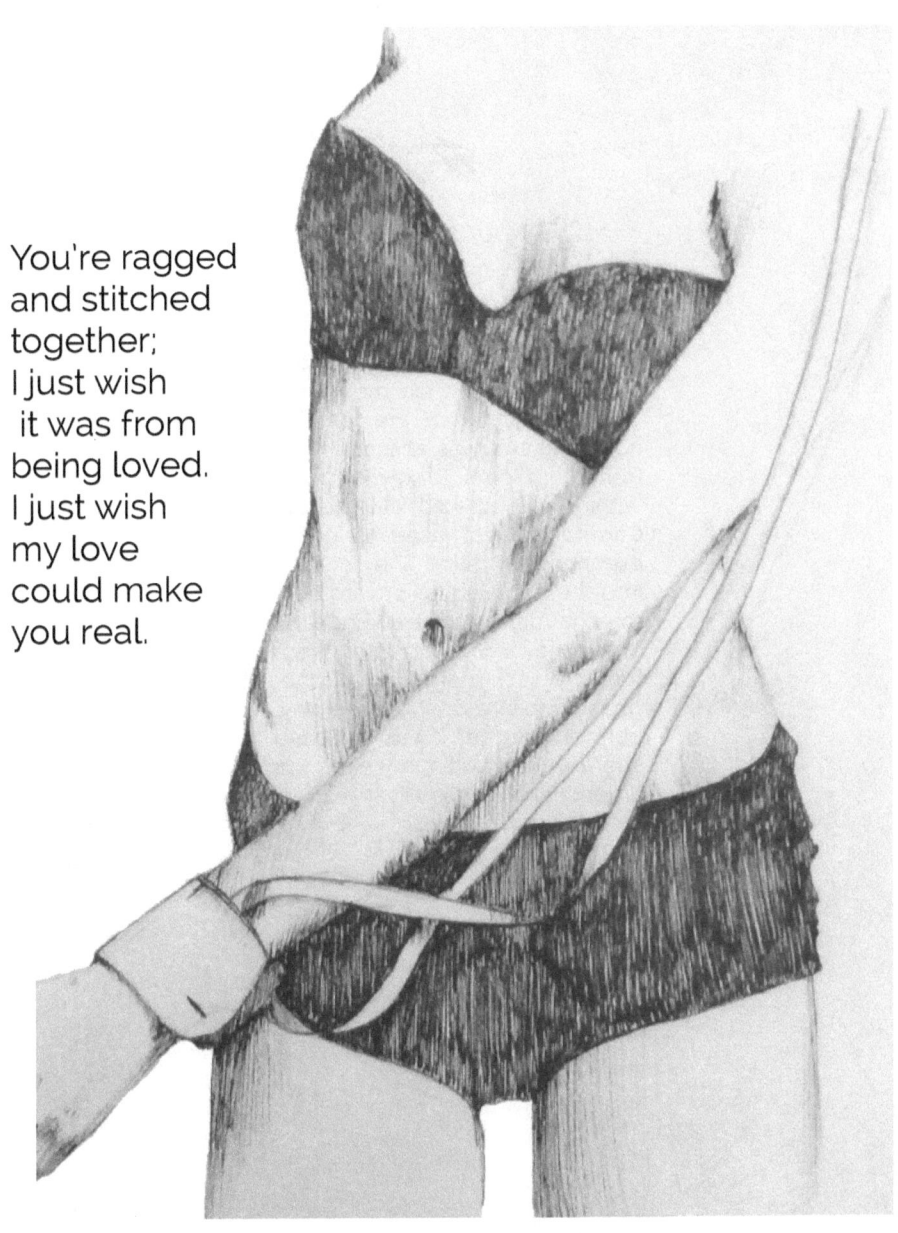

You're ragged
and stitched
together;
I just wish
 it was from
being loved.
I just wish
my love
could make
you real.

The Luna Zine
Gia - Sia Jane

#156

Joshua Dale

Her pale skin, bewitched by the waxing moon, engrossed my unknowing eye; her shadow casted upon me insidiously. she was the master of the forest for in the nude, her skin was enscribed in branches. Reflecting pool for eyes, was she, and within, I witnessed the life beyond.

Caressing what used to be my goose bump ridden skin, She took me deeply into the bowels of a private hell reserved for what cannot be explained. She lay me into my icy tomb with a sour kiss and the forest and I merged into one and my ghastly mistress straddled my spirit to oblivion's edge. I was doomed to ever see the light again; my eyes unclosed to an enchanting void reserved for her, what cannot be explained.

Surf
Thom Young

The surf
isn't what
it use to be
now
it
washes up
lives
and dirty needles
and once they found
a lady
in a green dress
face down on the beach.
she said her
name was Amber
which seemed like a good enough
name
but the tourists
were too distracted
by a school
of Bluefish
to know
they were
already eaten
alive.

The Only One
RD Johnson

Simple minded people
can bear simple minded souls
at the bottom of the barrel
like the bottom of our soles.
Use them as a stepping stone
when you think you the only one,
just know you're not alone.
There's many that go unnoticed.
There's many that don't know us.
There's many that go before their
time and they didn't get a chance
to show us everything that
they wanted, or what they ever could.
Let's pray for better days and
I'll even suffice for days that are good.
Now, I don't need for ya'll to
check completely out in
order for that to register.
You wanna be running the
show or the one behind the register.
You wanna be the loser or
the one being the competitor.
I strive to be extraordinary,
my vocabulary doesn't contain regular.

Have You Ever?
Joe Adomavicia

I wonder—
Have you ever taken the time to notice,
how Summer's sun can clear gunmetal skies,
or how it refracts off the water
of a somber heaven—
Filling the darkness behind your eyes?

I wonder—
Have you ever taken the time to notice,
how when Spring's roses begin to blossom
the wind carries love's scent through the air
or how it effortlessly enraptures—
permeating beauty
from within the pigment of it's petals?

I wonder—
have you ever taken the time to notice,
how the cycle of Autumn's leaves remain parallel
to the frailty of the living
or how the perpetuity of their purpose
is either known of and ignored or understood and accepted?

I wonder—
Have you ever taken the time to notice
how the Winter's deep freeze
blankets and preserves the earth beneath our feet
To walk upon in new years to come,
Or how it brings forth the warmth of family's serenity?

A Childhood Tale

Emma Charlton

Grazing my hands over
the dining table
I've eaten dinner at
almost every night of my life
the table that has
accompanied at least
one hundred hungry people
and left five
still hungry
and unsatisfied.

Not once has
the wood
bitten me and left me
with a splinter,
it has always been
too kind
to be like that.
Fixated by the knots
in the polished
red gum,
I am reminded
of a birthmark
you had on your elbow.
That one you told me you
were self-conscious
of but I thought
it was beautiful.
I still think
it is beautiful.

I let my eyes trail
past a thick dried sappy
bit of varnish,
and settle on a dent,
four separate holes
each horizontal,
in a perfectly straight line.

And I remember just exactly
how it got there.

On the last night of autumn,
not too long ago when
Anger and Frustration
exploded like stars, and you
told me I should not
do that.
That the only thing I should
let explode are the galaxies
beneath my skin.
But last night I let
that swirl down the drain,
but if I told you that you
would probably explode,
too.

I let my heart leap
enthusiastically
from my chest,
up through my throat
and out through my
mouth, like water did
that time I was in the
hospital for three days
with a severe case of
dehydration
that almost
got me.

And I let it plummet
itself into a fast descent
towards the polished
red gum table, and
when it landed,
the table became
a richer-than-ever
shade of crimson,
and I've never seen you so
shocked.
Not even
when I said a word, I've
only recently been taught
not to say I play with it.
Pushing it around with my
blunt knife and buckled fork.

The same way I do when
there is a single pea
drowning in the gravy
on my plate,
and never do I try
to save it because I don't
care. And maybe I should,
but I already took
what I wanted,
anyway.
It was in that moment
you told me
to stop playing
with my food.
I did not at all
have the guts
to tell you,
that maybe you shouldn't play
with my feelings when
I put them on the table.

Friday Night

Cassie Ferraro

I laid quietly, starving, anxious to feel anything. When he finally reached out, my body quivered, unfamiliar with the tender language. Words began to pour from his fingers, writing poetry down my spine, to my wrist. Our fingers intertwined, bringing the fragments into a whole. I opened softly, my binding tearing with each lovely sentence he penned with his hands. He moved emphatically, in decided ardor. There was nothing virtuous in his words, yet the essence so pure. Staccato breaths, a hyphen between thoughts relieved my rhythmic heartbeat. He wrote so quickly. I reluctantly stopped him. Inside I was bursting with a monologue that was screaming to be heard. I closed my eyes and let the words spill.
"How can I make you realize that I dive deeper than most?" I said, my voice stronger than I anticipated. "You see, I reach beyond the surface. I dive into that opaque navy. I'm not scared of the pressure, or the darkness. I embrace the things others fear. I'm not content to marvel in the shallow swells. I want to be carried in your currents." He was looking at me now, startled with my honesty. I kept going. "How can I make you realize that I feel this yearning to explore your depths while you're content to lie on my shore?" My voice quivered with obstinate truth. I tugged at the sheets and drew them close to wipe away the single tear that had rolled onto my cheek. He turned his head to stare at the ceiling. His body may as well have been across the world. We spent what felt like years, laying side by side like that. I resolved that this was the end of whatever we had begun and sat up. As soon as I moved, his arms found my waist. His touch was cautious and I felt the trepidation in his fingers. Yet, he pushed it aside and moved his hands slowly up my body to take my face to his.

And in one blink, an ephemeral ellipsis, his lips touched mine and the first chapter was written.

You
Randy Mascorro

You
and that sleepy voice
If I close my eyes
tight enough
I can still remember
those nights
you kept me
alive when
all I needed to
hear was you.

Dark Side (Pain From Within)
I. Wimana. C

I looked into the mirror and
saw once again my own fear
The only thing that has
had me running from it all these years.
But it won't leave, It won't quit, It's stuck in me
Eating and tearing away, Wanting to be let free.
My mind is losing its personality.
My heart is growing cold.
For the trapped rage in me is growing hard to hold.
I go through every day, calm, mellow and cool.
No tears I shed on the outside but inside me is a pool.
The walls are breaking, my very soul is aching,
My body is at its limit I'm getting more frustrated.
But I know I can't give in.
These scars must stay within.
But this feeling,
This anger,
It shows no sign of subsiding.
Like a bird without its wings.
Like a lion without its roar
I lost myself, my very being,
And began to be no more.
In one last attempt to regain
what was once mine
I shot my eyes and searched
within the very core of my mind.
Blood rushed through my veins,
My heart began pumping and
my senses awoke.
I opened my eyes an in front of me
was a person shielded in a dark cloak.
The room was in darkness.
I was being choked by the silence.
The air got dense I was struggling for my existence.
The stranger was not moving
but I felt as if he was ripping out my insides.
And I got this oh so familiar feeling
when I tried to look into his eyes.
It was the same feeling I got
when I looked in the mirror
and saw what I see.
A flash of lighting brightened the room...
And it...
It...
It was my fear...
It was me...

Transformation
Allison Greenlee

Sometimes, when words cannot capture meaning
In life, love, death, and what lies in between,
There are gestures that speak in depths of feeling
That need to be heard and not go unseen.

What speaks beyond human language is true -
Just like plucking heart strings to hear clearly;
One may begin to see from a new view,
That wake the souls of the lost and dreary.

When you have to learn to love and let go
Life is compared to a fading sunset;
Feeling all too surreal in time, although
The Sun reflects truth like a still vignette.

Live on like the ancient morphing Phoenix
That knows no loss from the power of Nyx.

Collide

LR Poetess

Our souls didn't collide. There were no fireworks that exploded and lit up our chests. Ours souls waved timidly at each other from a distance and instantly knew they could light up the sky brighter than a million stars.

Allison Greenlee
Photography

Beautiful Her
Randy Mascorro

Beautiful her
with eyes I get lost
in and I don't need
to be found
My god that
smile mends
me so it is impossible
to walk around broken.

Lucky
Harry Howard

I think I'm lucky,
while everyone
else is staring at
your body and
your curves,
I'm left with
your mind
all to myself,
and fuck is
it beautiful.

My fingers part my lips, and with another deep breath my heart - severed but intact - is in my hands once again.

The Luna Zine
Gia - Sia Jane

Lie to me like you love me
Brande Mcclees

Lie to me like you love me
As if your only thought at
the end of the day is being
wrapped up in me
Like all of the happily
ever after's of fairy tales
are possible.

Lie to me like
Shakespeare's tales of love.
Like Teddy Pendergrass' voice
and Dr. J's swoop.
Lie to me like you love me
purely Like chocolate's first kiss
And a freshly fallen snow
Or summer rain.

Tell me it all, but
know that I expect it to
Be a lie

Addicted

Kolleen Rianne

A beautiful canvas I was.
I was painted with color and I was vibrant.
I was full of life, strong minded until I met you. I became entangled in you. Lost in curiosity of life. I became so attached to your influence that I was drowning with questions.
I was engaged in your presence and drawn into you. You slowly sucked me into this whirlwind of the unknown and everything else that was colorful and vibrant became dark and over bearing. I had suddenly lost me. I was gone in seconds. No pulse. I could hear myself yelling, screaming but nothing. I laid there for someone. But you took over my mind.

You drew me in and I was stuck on you.
You became the drug I never wanted and didn't need, but when I had you, I felt like I was alive. Whatever was left of me, you had. That beautiful canvas that was once painted colorful and vibrant was no longer filled with such. My curiosity for you left marks on my heart, my body and my spirit. You destroyed me, whatever life was left of me. Sad part is, I let you destroy me.

I am stronger now. I know longer need you.
My curiosity for you has vanished and my mind is stronger than my needs for you. I will not let you take what is left of me because my life is more important than losing everything because of you.

Charmaine Landwehr

I think people forget, forget what it's like to connect Connect with someone on a spiritual sense. To not see race or religion but see what's standing in front of them without the stigma the disillusion . The false illusion of what people pretend to be, We forget the solution. The conscious revolution. The way to overthrow the governments, The way to free our souls of the whole stupid constitution. Most of us don't want to see it, we close our eyes live blindly and disconnect scared of our own resolution. Anything to escape the damn confusion of our minds realizing what they don't want us to see, seeing the cracks in their perfectly put together lies, something deep inside encouraging us to look into it further to bring about better days where we awaken to a peaceful conclusion. To stand together as one and take on all that is wrong. They don't want us to see the power, the power with us. The power that can stop a nation. Stop there very corrupt institution.

Pause breathe in, we can change this world grab somebody's hand let's cause a global fusion. To unite as one and finally end what could very well be the end-
humanity's mass execution..

The Eruption of Vesuvius
Valorie Kristen Ruiz

a   city   buried
                 under   ash
                         restless.
                      men   almost forgotten
                           But
                               the sky
                                      dust and
                   fields   lived
after

time.

Driven to Madness

Arnab Bose

Would it be fair to tell you, at times I realize you deserve better but I won't let you slip away from me in my selfishness. Would an act of crime such as that be pardoned by something such as love? Keeping you tied to me with the knot between your lips, every moment they meet.
Encaging you within a grasp that tries to satisfy your desires and yet possesses the fragility to calm your senses. Freezing you in time away from existence with the cold touch of a gaze you'd be in a prison. And a prison shelters the seed of insanity. Driven to madness within which you may think to harm yourself on any patch of skin left untouched by your oppression, if you were not already chained away from the possibility of the thought.
A mixture of opposing tears may dilute your vision of the future, but I assure it will remain as clear as ever if you remain in my bonds.

So tell me, would a crime such as this be forgiven in the name of love?

Lovers Land
Gloria Linares

My heart is complete.
My soul feels serene.
Wasteful arguments
decreased, respect
became our priority.
Placing our love above
anything else.
Nobody exists
when we're alone
in lovers land.

Hope
Almaz Azmi

I hope you understand that sometimes I cannot lift this troubled soul of mine to be the strong person you always thought I was. So forgive me, love, if I ask to crawl into your embrace every once in a while. Forgive me, for showing you the weary stains on my bones.

Nothing Lasts Forever
The Typist

The nothings become
something. Or someone.
Or the universe. And 'forever'
was just a made up word the
watchmakers used to borrow
more time. Maybe being
tangled in the politics
of time and dimensions
is the philosophy keeping
us slaves to this gravity.

If I could just break
the clocks I would float
forever in the electric abyss;
if I could just break all the clocks.

Never been the girl next door

Valorie Kristen Ruiz

Not the type of woman to be called baby girl.
I walk and leave scorched heel marks.
I've got half a sleeve of tattoos over scars
more painful than the ink stained art.

But when you said Baby Girl I caved, crumbled,
bent over spineless to hear you mumble it once
more.

I was never one to fall for your red wine love:
I'm a bitter IPA. I play with cuffs and pretend
not to like your fingers trailing my thighs or
gentlemen style ties: satin pushing my skin,
you whisper Say when

But with you I became effervescent champagne
in your hands caught in glass: bubbling up,

pouring over, for a touch of your mouth.

Pierced
The Typist

It was pierced,
at the tip – her tongue.
Native, like her olive skin.
I didn't know her language, but I
could tell, it too had been pierced
by a different kind of metal.
And so I asked her,
the way to the graveyard, where
mother tongues go to die.

To the loved ones
Mackenzie Mullen

I am falling from where
once was saved and
the question remains
If I will ever feel the
serenity that I had felt
above the clouds.
I am left with a
disconsolate window of
misfortune and Despair,
For now disaster
follows me where
I once laid my head
and called my home.
I cannot search for
peace and hope
for the ones who
outcasted me are
everywhere.
I feel their stare lurking
through my windows
at night. I hear their
voices calling me hauntingly.
My feet have frozen from
the cold, hard, ground
I am now forced
to walk Upon.
By God, it's nothing
 like the clouds.
If you have ever had the
opportunity to walk With
Angels in their home,
You would know Nothing
can ever make You
feel as good as that.
Now I am forced to repent
In a world so dark and lonely.
Tell me, To the ones
who once Loved me
dearly, why is it
you who have hurt
me the worst.

Girl of Dreams
Neithan Levi

Looking around the
corner, I think I see her.
The girl of my dreams,
the girl of my life.

She is beautiful, but her
beauty does not matter.
Like music would do to a
composer, the sound of her
laughter fills my soul.
Her heartbeat vibrates
through my chest
like the sound of mellow
drums.

Her hair falls lovely down
her face exactly as the river
flows.

Stars
Ramsha Zubairi

to all the stars
that have returned back
to the night sky (where
you've always belonged)
and shine bright (like
you were always meant
to) you are missed by
all those who knew you,
by all those you thought
wouldn't miss you.

Surrender
The girl with Kaleidoscope Heart

Surrender my dear.
Make memories that
live forever. Let the
lust consume us like
alcohol, surrender whole.
Surrender all. Let's write
another story of true love,
different than the rest.
Let our love speak.
Urge for the best.
Surrender your soul to me,
we'll travel to the stars
and sail the sea.
Surrender and walk
with me towards the light,
forget the wrongs.
Forget what isn't right.
Drop your weapons
and leave your armor,
let the burning fire of love spread
through your body.
Get rid of all the things
that pull you back.
And walk with me
to those lush green
meadows, nothing
follows us there.
Not even our shadows.
Alone. Together. We will
make love there.

Rhett Pritchard/S.L. Foxton

This Place

S.W Collins

I stare at the celling, with swollen red eyes for lack of sleep. I roll on the bed, noticing the emptiness of it, The lack of warmth in the place you used to lay your dreams on. I myself feel a hole deep in my chest, Where your love fulfilled me,
A broken organ that's called heart,
This place you used to live in.
This place now in flames and burning,
This place, this house of ancient loves,
So fucked up, so rotten.

Diagnostics
S.L. Foxton

Engine stalled out, clunking against
what seemed to be the wheel wells
and shaking hands with tire treads
to vibrate arms, cheeks, brain,
just as I pulled into the driveway.
I heard something funny
a few miles into cruise control,
a snickering of joke-telling,
must have been somewhere near the fan belt,
but recent circumstances and the egregious notion
that cars can heal themselves
told me to go on.
  But alas, I've sputtered and spiraled
into homebound, motherland runway
next to the pickup I suppose I'll be using
so long as graces are good.
  The beast dies with quieter and quieter
revolutions per minute.
I told my friend I'd drive it into the ground,
until the wheels fell off or the engine block exploded,
but this seems less dramatic than I'd hoped
as the last of the clanking subsides.
  Mechanic would later tell me there was absolutely zero
oil in the reservoirs
and ask how I'd been running this long
before offering $1500
just to take it off my hands.
  Hesitant to reserve the last few years of my life
to the scrap heap,
but he assures me his intentions are pure
when the difference between cost for parts
and cost for parts and labor is explained.
Still, the idea of it running around town
in certified pre-owned condition,
not a hiccup in the transmission,
irked me more than the thought of seeing it compressed
down under extreme pressure
into a cube a quarter of the size
though density would remain.
  Mechanic would later tell me he was able to gut
everything and replace it with newness,
and that if I saw it on the street
I'd hardly recognize it,
which I suppose is for the better.

Feelings

The girl with Kaleidoscope Heart

I see the stars fall,
I see the sky cry,
I see the sun burn in rage,
I see the moon wane,
I see the storm's insanity,
I see the waves reaching out,
I hear the winds scream,
I feel the anguish of thunder....
Yes...I see, I feel And I hear.... Their feelings

One More Surgery
Huma Adnan

"See, you check her up and if there is no need of operation then just give her medicine." Nasreen, a bulky lady wrapped in light brown shawl, insisted.
Sister, why don't you understand that your daughter's condition isn't good enough that we can take more risk?
"She never had any health problem. Ma Sha Allah (By God's grace) she eats well and we have been taking her treatment from Dr. Rauf" She said.
Listen try to understand that Dr. Rauf has been giving her drug nicorandil (a potassium-channel activator) for hypertension due to which her condition has gone worse. Has she had issue of hyper tension?
"No, she answered hurriedly and continued, but he said if we would operate her so in future she might not be able to conceive,"
Oh Lord! There isn't such thing. Doctor lost his patient and tried to explain her the process, First, we will insert a tube in her anal with small camera. If heaven forbids she has colectral cancer which I have presumed, we have to operate her immediately.
"hmm.. all right, I will call my son now and discuss this matter with him."
Means? He asked surprisingly.
"oh he lives in Germany." She replied proudly.
So she is yours? He asked while looking at Shazia.
"She is my daughter in law." She said loudly than usual.
Really? She was calling you Ama so I couldn't judge.
Nasreen frowned a little and replied hastily, "Han I also call her beti, daughter. She is our daughter.
She pulled Shazia towards her and held her tightly in arms. She kissed her face several time and giggled. Shazia, who was sitting quietly during all that conversation, got startled. It didn't take her long to accept the sudden shower of love as it was a norm which often took place in front of acquaintances. But her weak fragile body which was stick to bed shivered with such unexpected gesture. But her mind was working faster than body and it seemed as that her brain was not attached with the same body. It was least affected by the illness. There was overflow of unstoppable thoughts which were pricking her like thorns. She was someone who used to get scared from hospital door was today screaming in her heart to cut open her, to dissect her, to chop her, but at least set her free from that unbearable pain. The pain which she has been bearing from last seven days has now spread to each and every vein and nerve. All she wanted was a cure! A freedom! A peace!

But it was still not decided that was she most needed by the people who were connected to her or the fetus which hasn't even been sown in her barren womb.
"Beta, Child, have you spoken to Imran?"
No, not yet, Ami, mother.
"It's okay, he must be busy. You go for operation. We will inform him once we speak to him."

I just want to listen to his voice then I would go.
"Hah! You don't worry, we will contact and inform him. We have to call him to send money for your operation." Nasren replied with frustration.
But just two days ago bhai, my brother sent fifty thousand rupees. It would be enough to pay the hospital bills.
"Which 25,000?? We have spent all on your medication and service. Don't worry my Imran will return each and every penny back." She said furiously.
Shazia was in dilemma either to say something or stay quiet that suddenly nurse entered and announced while handling her light blue gown,
Wear this and then I will bring wheel chair. First we will test the blood.
Just give me one minute. I don't need a wheel chair. I will walk, just give me one minute. She pledged.
Nurse didn't seem to mind her request and she left quietly. Shazia started dialing Imran's number impatiently. As usual the recording was being played in German and the very first word was enough to understand that the phone was switched off. She didn't know the meaning of a single word but for her it sounded as someone was shouting in her ears and saying, "Your call isn't important!"
Finally she gave up and left a text message for Imran,
"I am going to be operated in a while. I really need you. My phone will be off."
The pain which aroused in her heart was far more intense than the physical pain for which she was being taken to operation theatre. It was hard to switch off her phone as sometimes the simple little decisions are like a slow poison which drill the hole in heart so deep that it not only drains the love but the loved ones too. While she was occupied with her thoughts she heard a voice,
Give your hand we need to insert cannula into your vein.
Suddenly all her fears were gone, nervousness was replaced with a strange smile. She started looking the process in which needles were inserted in her veins. When the nurse was trying to find the vein she looked at her face to see sooth her if she has been in pain, but she was forced to exchange the smile and were wondering what was making Shazia so glad. All the preparations were completed for this Medical ritual but the person who was supposed to light the torch was not there.
She could recall the days when she would sleep in late and listen to all the songs of vital signs a famous Pakistani band in 90s. Her friends would often tease her for her choice. All in sudden she could feel herself back in her home, at midnight typing her assignment while listening to Junaid Jamshed's song Mar Jau Tou, If I die..
Suddenly the voice started chanting again in her ears,

Mar bhi jau tou mat rona
Beeti hui bato ko,
Jagi hui rato ko
Yad karna aur jee lena

If I die, do not cry
Recall the gone things,
And awake nights,
And live again.

All she wanted to know dressed in blue gown and with pale face if there would be someone to cry for her.
After the completion of all the medical ritual she was taken to a cold room and was asked to lie down on flat hard table. It was unlike her expectations; as cold as the hearts of people waiting outside and colder than that particular night of February.
Suddenly the seed of negativity sowed in her mind and it started growing its roots, trunk and stems. Her soul started inviting all the demons and slowly the maleficent thoughts started circling her. To escape the darkness in the bright room she started looking around her. But she felt her feet being lifted and tied. She lifted her head to see and found the nurse in white dress tying the feet with the table.
Why are you tying me? She asked.
Silence was the answer.
Am I going to move during sleep? She asked again.
Silence once again.
She turned her head right and saw a clean shaved man with glasses on his nose almost 45 years old was busy in reading a humungous book. He was Surgeon Faisal and was known as passionate doctor who never had a case which went wrong. To fight her demons she tried to communicate with him.
What are you reading?
He never answered and it reminded her of all those Chinese science fiction movies which she would watch during her vacation to kill her boredom. In those movies there would always be some secret mission in which scientist performed some experiment on their specimen in the laboratory.
So even sci-fi is based on reality. She thought.
The third person to enter in the room was the same doctor who advised her parents in law to operate her immediately. He came near to her and placed his hand on her forehead like a caring and concerned father and softly said.
"Don't be scared beta, my child."
Those words seemed to hurt her ego and she promptly replied,
I'm not scared!
Nothing was truer than that; she wasn't scared of being cut and opened. They weren't needles and scissors which were scaring her, those were her demons whispering the unseen in her ears and alarming her for something which hadn't happened.
Why have you tied me with this table?
"So that you mightn't run in your sleep." The doctor answered with kind smile.
Have you watched the movie The Awake?
For a moment the doctor was startled at this sudden question and then he replied,

"Umm no. Why?"

In that movie there was a surgery of a boy but he had anesthesia awareness during the operation. He felt each and everything which was done to him. His body was paralyzed but his brain never slept.
The doctor smiled again and said,
"But my child that was just a film."
After watching that film I read on the internet that it does happen. There are some people who experienced it. She replied.
"But you will sleep my child."
What if I didn't? She asked persistently.
To keep her nerves calm doctor gave her a smile in answer to this question. The surgeon who was occupied with the book removed his glasses and kept closed the book. He walked to the table and asked her,
"What was the name of that film?"
The Awake. She answered.

He took out his phone and typed something and put it back in his pocket.
Who is going to give me anesthesia? She asked from surgeon.
"Doctor Adil." The surgeon replied while looking towards that father-like doctor.
Why? Why there is no staff for anesthesia? She was surprised.
"Beta, my child, this is government hospital. We don't have much staff like private hospitals."
She understood his point well. She realized that in 20,000Rp this was all she could have. She was no more in her father's house where she would be taken to city's expensive hospitals even if she had minor fever. It is strange that luck showers more money on blood relations than others. Perhaps, visible money.
"Why do you speak so much? Think of Allah, God." Surgeon advised.
Allah is already here. She replied.
Doctor moved at the back of her head to adjust something and said,
"Read Kalima*"

Why? Am I not going to wake up? She asked.
"You will." And he brought some pipe near to her face and tried to adjust something which she couldn't see.
"Come on read Kalima."
La illaha illalu Muhammadur rasool Allah. "He is Allah, [who is] One, Allah, the Eternal Refuge. He neither begets nor is born, nor is there to Him any equivalent." She read softly.
"That's it?" He asked again.
Yeah that's it. I have short Kalima. My mom had the longer one.
"Okay. Recite again." He laughed.
And suddenly the fog appeared in front of her eyes. She felt the colors fading in front of her eyes. Something strange occupied her brain either dizziness or nausea but she couldn't figure that out anymore. The peace didn't stay long; it was replaced with 'anesthesia awareness'. She started moving but soon felt the pain in her abdomen. She could smell everything stinking around her. The two faces on her top grew bigger than before with every other thing, there

masks, their eyes and theatrical lights.
She heard the voice screaming in her ears,
"Doctor! Anesthesia!"
She couldn't remember anything after that.
Once she got up she was being moved from Operation Theater to ward. She could see people standing in corridor staring at her, some with pity eyes and some with curiosity. It seemed for an instance they forgot the purpose that why they were standing in those long corridors of the hospital. This is such a mystery that what pleasure do people get in staring at the faces of helpless ones.
Why a human has so much curiosity to see the pain of others. During time of tragedies everyone turns into the news reporter who tries to be strong while doing the coverage of
calamities. The only difference is that such people try to grasp as much as they could to convey eye-witnessed events to the other people from their tongue rather through satellite. For them being a witness is no less than an achievement, they find consider it as an addition to their life's experience.
Among the crowd she tried to search for a familiar face which didn't exist there. But this time she didn't crave for Imran, her lips uttered an unfamiliar name.
Abd-ull-ah!
"My beti, daughter, we will just call Imran." A lady whispered in typical mellifluous voice to keep the masquerade alive.
NO!! Abdul.. She tried to scream but vomited.
Nasreen looked at her angrily and turned to her husband,
"Who the hell is Abullah? I will just call Imran and ask him to divorce this whore!"
Before Nasreen's husband could open the mouth, doctor interrupted,
"It was a right decision to operate her else the cancer would have spread."
The cancer wasn't cure it had just started to grow inside her soul and in her life. This time money wasn't enough for any other surgery.

Withered
LR Poetess

My imperfections
break and crack
my skin
and I peel them off
my face
like old withered paint
to reveal my new
but still flawed self.
I am still learning
to be the best version
of me I can be.
Please love,
be patient and gentle with me.

Snapshot of December 14

S.L. Foxton

I have died
during several celebrations.
I have seen
several raptures come to pass
and several judgment days postponed
on account of a hung jury.
I have stopped
coming to breakfast with my shoelaces untied
and opted out of shoes entirely before 10
for the remainder of the year.
I have grown
into a pair of leather boots
that used to be my father's, but have been sitting
ignored in a corner of the hall closet
for seven winters now.
I have stumbled
upon Junior's comic book collection
in another closet
entombed in a beige file box
and became fascinated at how each was sealed
and uncontaminated in their little plastic bags
and felt my first impulse toward preservation.
I have looked
timidly over the vinyl collection every night
for two years and 47 days and have remembered
all 750 titles, in alphabetical order
and according to personal rank,
as well as his Top 100 judging by play-through frequency.
I have chatted
with you on the roof just outside my window
and we spoke of the quality of certain things at hand
and you joked about falling off, then almost did,
but it was me who wound up landing on a car,
halving myself over the windshield,
Half for you
Half for me
Half for medical expenses
and you told me I was probably concussed at the very least.
I have smoked
entire bonfires trying to keep the thing lit
through the night,
throwing on logs when needed,
stoking when needed,
spraying helpings of lighter fluid when needed
and still fell asleep and woke to dying coals.
I have fainted
several times simply on account
of remembering that I was still awake.

I have lived
in several aftermaths

Plight
Sarah Murdock

How is it my hands seize
what I cannot unearth?

This mind is not made of clay;
you cannot mold it,
you cannot

you cannot.

I am tired,
so worn with sifted uncertainty
though I see it all so clear

the tactile remains
of a once buoyant being,

an anomaly asserting sovereignty sits;
you cannot persuade it,
you cannot

you cannot.

Once,
I dreamt of seas so still
they calmed a storm.

Nostalgia
Shannan Wiltshire

Nostalgia burns me
crisp and tinted in
cider gold
I rumble for that
peached youth;
I peel my skin
back looking for it,
all to lather the
shreds back together
in morning sea salt
when once again
I find nothing

Bottomless Top Hats
Samantha Lasky

She sat in the back of the room
Her name was the many syllables of words she got called.
Strung together in a hiss.
Nobody
loser
ugly
stupid.
She believed in so much more than she let on.
There were good things in the world
or so she told herself.
But there wasn't anyone to second that.
The girl thought bottomless hats were the secret to magic tricks,
and if she could crawl around in the dark
eventually a magician would pull her out
for the whole world to ooh and ahh.
Fantasies.
But the quiet corner she occupied
was not as mystical as black top hats.
And she knew there was no other way to escape
beyond a portal
stepping into another life.
Because buses and trains weren't for her.
The short distances they covered
were so unlike the millions of miles of a different world.
The one a magician held in his outstretched fingers.
Stupid.
If she searched long enough in the light,
she could feel the edges of loneliness curling in
like the rim of a paper set aflame
reminding her of where she was
making her face the circle of people she was ridiculed by.
There was so much to be ashamed of,
and often so little to be relieved about.
Ugly.
It was like trying to escape the same torture
every second.
The bullies had their magic, too.
And it was a dirty trick they played on her,
again and again.
The girl was a lovely assistant behind bars.

Didn't smile pretty
and instead stood behind the playground smoking cigars.
Her shimmering outfit reduced to rags,
the tatters of her black dress swinging in the breeze
with kids laughter rolling across the tips of trees
the glitter on her eyes now smears of blood,
Why didn't she get to be the star of the show?
Where was her spot light?
Forgotten.
The air of the night always ran cold
she flipped the light switch but it filled the streets with shadows,
and she hoped the wind would snuff it out.
The bullies had tricks up to their elbows–
they thrived on deception and slight of hand.
Just a kick here
a puckered lip there
and later all the lies that followed.
Weak.
No Ms. M, Kathy tripped on the sidewalk playing hop scotch.
And so all those little white lies got bigger.
Kathy was always trying
trying to jump far enough to reach the road
where she was sure the hands of her bullies couldn't reach for her
because even they had their boundaries.
And didn't chase her lest they no one was looking.
Friendless.
The bubble of protection behind locked bathroom doors–
The safe haven she created–
could be infiltrated at any second.
But she tried to make it her own,
not to think about that.
Propped up books and cast a blanket
like a canopy.
Swung her legs over the edge
and pointed her fingers at the accusers.
Wasn't sure if they could find her–
made a cage out of solitude,
counted the seconds down to the end of the day.
She stood opposite them at recess,
laughing with her back turned
so they couldn't see her ability to smile.
They haven't beaten me yet.
And yes the sidewalks have seen more of her than the mirror
and sure the swings on the set had quite a long story to tell
but they are quiet.
Hush hush,
because nobody wanted to hear it.
Loser.

The truth was kept in hearts crossed with lies.
And the wand that locked the spell was tossed aside.
The box she stepped in was way too small,
too small to get lost in.
The darkness clamps her fingers down
and the lid of the box is screwed on too tight
the toes on her feet are tucked in like curbs.
All she wants to do is see the next day
before the abracadabra sends her down the rabbit hole.
Hope.
Where will Kathy go when she reaches the end?
When just like her bullies, she sees magic is pretend?
How lost can one feel when put in the dark,
knowing they're going into the mouth of a shark?
Strong.
The bullies stand above her
rooting around in their bottomless top hats.
But the bunny they can't find fell through a different trap.
And the lovely assistant blows smoke into rings,
she stands like a survivor, wearing tattered old things.
But she has a story
her smile does hol
the one that the swords in her heart have already told.
She raises a hand
to the rightfully accused.
Telling them magic never works,
when it's wrongfully misused.

Neglected Love
Kolleen Rianne

Our love was beautiful,
magical for the most part.
Then slowly but
surely we lost it.
We became so in
tuned with our lives
that we forgot
to include one another.
We forgot to date one
another, rekindling
the flame, keeping the spark.
We forgot to show and
give affection that it became
so normal for us.
We forgot about each other.
My love for her
was still strong
but I was not in
love with her anymore.
Her love for me showed,
but it was not in ways where
I knew as a man,
I stole her heart
every day and made her
continuously fall in love
with me over and over again.
When she loved me,
I neglected her heart.
When I loved her, she
lost my attention.
We forgot how to
love one another.
That's when we realized,
we lived as roommates
and not lovers.

Celestial
The Typist

Fanatics of curiosity
Not of gods, scripture
Or some celestial authority.
We belong to the religion of question marks
Of stubborn science and the darkest arts.

Radicals of a violence called Zen.

ARTIST BIO

Arnab Bose

I'm a 20 year old aspiring writer and musician, who tries his best to understand the world. I'm just another puzzle piece trying to change the bigger picture.

L R Poetess

Dear beautiful being,
Let me tell you why I've decided to be anonymous. I choose to remain faceless because these words, they aren't my words alone. They are yours too. These stories are your stories too. I want you to be able read a piece of mine and say "Yes! This is what has been living inside me! This is what I've been trying to say!" I want to be the one who writes down the words you sometimes can't seem to find. I want to be the one who writes down what you've never had the courage to say. I want you to be able to send a piece of mine to your loved one without having to associate my face with it. I want you to see yourself in the words that I put out. Whether you're in love or heartbroken or a little bit of both, this is for you because I am you.

Jeremy Tolbert

Jeremy M. Tolbert is a poet and writer from Seattle, WA. He has written for the Seattle Post-Intelligencer online, The Original Van Gogh's Ear Anthology, Having a Whiskey Coke With You and a few others. He has penned two poetry collections, Scribblings from a Beer-Stained Napkin and Talking with the Devil About Love, both out by University Bookstore Press. His third collection, I'd Catch Butterflies, will be out in 2017 by Rad Press Publishing.

Thom Young

Thom Young is a writer from Texas. His work has been in The Commonline Journal, 3am magazine, Crack the Spine, Word Riot, 48th Street Press, and many other places.

Ashley O'Melia

Ashley O'Melia is an independent author and freelancer from Southern Illinois. She has released several books, including The Wanderer's Guide to Dragon Keeping and The Graveside Detective. Her most recent short story, "Home," was published in The Penmen Review. Her freelancing experience includes ghostwriting, blogging, proofreading, beta reading, and social media marketing. She has worked for clients in numerous countries, including Germany, England, Israel, Canada, and the Netherlands. When Ashley isn't busy writing, gardening, or taking care of her family and pets, she can often be found curled up with a good book.

Brandon Tomlinson

I am a 24 year old history student from Jacksonville, Florida. My postal Address is as stated below

Brande Mcclees

Brande McCleese is a mama's girl, poet, blogger, animal lover, foodie, shoe addict and professor. The New Jersey native currently resides in North Carolina.

Joseph R. Adomavicia

Joseph R. Adomavicia at twenty four years old resides in Waterbury, Connecticut. His full time occupation is a licensed CNC (computer numerical control) Machinist at Edward Segal Incorporated. He is currently a student at Naugatuck Valley Community College pursuing an Associate Degree in Mechanical Engineering and also is pursuing an Associate Degree in Liberal Arts and Sciences. Aside from being one of the editors of Naugatuck Valley Community College's Fresh Ink magazine, the past two years his two poems Cerulean Wings and On Average, America were selected for publication. As for his poetry, it is diverse and stylistically intrinsic to the subject matter. As a writer his means are to portray generosity, inspiration and to be inspired by others. Within his words there are several glimpses of various aspects of life varying from love in its many faces, politics, poems of motivation and inspiration to the natural beauty of the world. He writes with the undying purpose to tell his times through his story written evocatively, inspiringly flowing free for the world to see.

Gloria Linares

Hello my name is Gloria L., I reside in sunny California. Writing poetry has always been a passion of mine. Just recently I decided to share it with everyone. If you'd like, feel free to browse through my writing on instagram @everlastingpoems. Hope you enjoy my words!

Cassie Ferraro

Cassie Ferraro works for Anthropologie, channeling her creativity into fashion and display. When she's not covered in paint or safety pins, she spends her time on her vintage Remington typewriter, hiking with her friends, and daydreaming about her next adventure. Despite having a background in political science, she has an unyielding passion for the arts and connecting with people through the written word.

Emma Charlton

"Seventeen year old Emma, a high school student, spends a majority of her time indulging in the therapeutic qualities of writing her own and reading others' poetry and prose. Emma is an idealist, part-time optimist and a creator. She one day hopes to publish her own book."

Rhett Pritchard

S.L. Foxton willed himself into existence, yet he doesn't actually exist in the human sense. He's been pacing around rooms for nearly a thousand years. Prior to that, he was no more than an otherworldly, out-of-body experience trying to figure out how to insert himself into various human forms. Since taking control of this particular vessel, he's decided to try his hand at the human art of writing. His first book is a collection of poems entitled Nausea and Nostalgia.

R.D Johnson

Reggie Johnson is a young poet out of Cincinnati, Ohio. At the age of 9, he picked up writing during family vacations, but now the passion is bigger than he could ever imagined. Reggie Johnson has released 2 chapbooks on Amazon, Strength In Numbers and Thin Rhymes Between Love & Hate, and is currently working on his third chapbook.

Huma Adnan

Huma Adnan was born in Quetta, Pakistan. She was the first woman of her family who rebelled against the system and stepped into university. She did her bachelors in English and moved to Dubai in 2011 with her husband. She works there as a language corporate trainer and has published a chapbook Verses From East. Currently, she is working on her full length book which reflects the culture and emotions of the society she was raised in.

Tania Brown

dearabbyisdead.com

Valorie K. Ruiz

Valorie K. Ruiz is a self-proclaimed bibliophile, multi-lingual, and fascinated with trees.

Shannan Wiltshire

Shannan Wiltshire is a student of English Literature and History at the University of Waikato, New Zealand.

Charmaine Landwehr

21 year old Australian artist
I believe language is the one thing that binds us. I write my feelings out on to paper hoping that just maybe one person can resonate within those words and relate. This is my passion and I hope maybe you feel that through my words - Charmaine Landwehr

The Girl With Kaleidoscope Heart

Tuhina Dave is currently studying law. She first experimented with writing by composing songs. Her hobbies include reading, writing and relaxing on the beach. Her dream is to travel the world. You can follow her on instagram - thegirlwithkaleidoscopeheart for more

Wimana Chadband

Imo Chadband, known to the writing world as I. Wimana. C, is an up and coming writer/poet hailing from the beautiful island of Trinidad and Tobago located in the Caribbean. Currently, he is working on a number of projects, the most recent being publishing his first book "The Puzzle: Finding That Missing Peace." His writing is real, raw, and passionate, gripping the reader as they resonate with words dripping with emotion. He can be contacted via email at i.wimana.c@hotmail.com. His writing, poetry, and updates to his projects can be found on:
instagram.com/i_wimana_c
facebook.com/IMO.IAmOriginal
twitter.com/i_wimana_c
iwimanac.tumblr.com

Samantha Lasky

My name is Samantha Claire Lasky. I am 15 years old and live in Chicago, Illinois. I've written words down since I could speak them! I hope in the future my writing will make a difference to people. I write because when I don't, I feel lost to the whims of the world around me. It seems like everyone just wanders by in life--and I don't think that will ever be enough for me. So I use words to find a way out.

www.ingramcontent.com/pod-product-compliance
Lightning Source LLC
Chambersburg PA
CBHW032049290426
44110CB00012B/1015